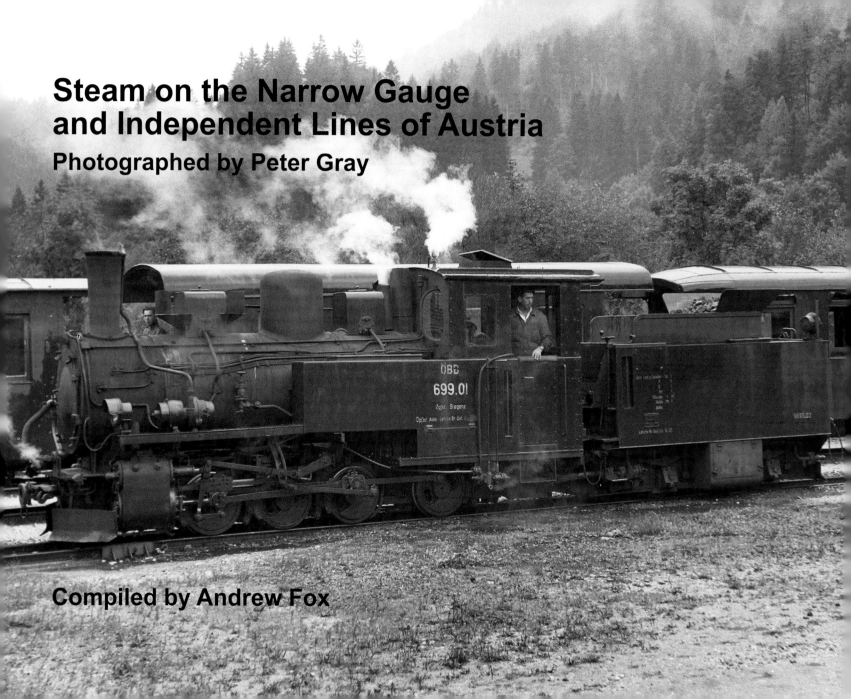

Steam on the Narrow Gauge and Independent Lines of Austria
Photographed by Peter Gray

Compiled by Andrew Fox

© Images and design: Peter Gray / The Transport Treasury 2021. Text Andrew Fox

ISBN 978-1-913893-05-7

First Published in 2021 by Transport Treasury Publishing Ltd. 16 Highworth Close, High Wycombe, HP13 7PJ

Totem Publishing, an imprint of Transport Treasury Publishing.

www.ttpublishing.co.uk
Printed in the UK by Henry Ling Limited, at the Dorset Press, Dorchester, DT1 1HD.

'Steam on the Narrow Gauge and Independent Lines of Austria' is one of a series of books on specialist transport subjects published in strictly limited numbers and produced under the Totem Publishing imprint using material only available at The Transport Treasury.

Front Cover: (1) Zillertalbahn No. 2 leaves Uderns with its train of seven four-wheel coaches and a van, and heads up the valley for Mayrhofen in the fading evening light of 12 September 1958. PG1641

Frontispiece: (2) Seen at Eisenkappel, terminus of the Vellachtalbahn, Class 699 0-8-0TT No. 699.01, originally Heeresfeldbahn No. HF 2818, was one of three Class KDL 11 locomotives which the ÖBB retained in their original tender-tank form. PG3510

Opposite: (3) The first of the six members of ÖBB Class 399, No. 399.01, built by Krauss, Linz in 1906 as Niederösterreichische Landesbahnen No. Mh 1, stands outside the shed at Gmünd, centre of the Waldviertelbahn narrow gauge system, on 1 September 1963. PG3417

Rear cover: (84) Two freights stand at Deutschlandsberg, with its distinctive signalbox, on the Graz-Köflacher Bahn line from Lieboch to Wies-Eibiswald on 4 September 1963. On the left is 2-8-0 No. 56.3253, built by Wiener Neustadt in 1919, and on the right is 2-6-2T No. 30.109, an StEG product of 1900. PG3476

Introduction

Peter Gray travelled to Austria several times in the 1950s and 1960s, notably as a participant in the 1958 and 1963 Railway Correspondence & Travel Society (RCTS) Austrian tours, visiting most of the country's steam operated narrow gauge lines, as well as the standard gauge Graz Köflacher Bahn with its remarkable collection of vintage second-hand locomotives, and the Steiermärkische Landesbahnen line from Gleisdorf to Weiz.

Peter's first visit to Austria, in July 1956, included the much-lamented Salzkammergut-Lokalbahn, which would close the following year. Despite the introduction of diesels on a number of lines in the 1930s, steam power was still dominant on most of the lines at the time of his visits, but would soon largely be displaced with the arrival of powerful new diesels. Over subsequent years many of Austria's narrow gauge railways would suffer progressive cut-backs and closure; Peter Gray's fine photographs provide a valuable record of a world that all too soon would disappear.

Whilst the majority of Austria's passenger-carrying narrow gauge lines were at this time operated by the nationalised Österreichische Bundesbahnen (ÖBB), those in the state of Steiermark (Styria) in the south-east of the country belonged to the regional Steiermärkische Landesbahnen (StmLB). In addition, the Austrian narrow gauge scene was enriched by three independent lines - the Salzkammergut-Lokalbahn, Zillertalbahn and Achenseebahn. With the exception of three metre gauge rack lines, all of the narrow gauge railways featured on the following pages operated on the near-universal Austrian narrow gauge of 760mm.

Salzkammergut-Lokalbahn

The famous 760mm gauge Salzkammergut-Lokalbahn (SKGLB) opened in stages between 1890 and 1893. The completed line, with a total length of 39½ miles (63.2km), ran from Salzburg to Bad Ischl, connecting with standard gauge lines at both ends, with a short branch from St Lorenz to Mondsee. Despite continuing high levels of traffic and strong local opposition, the SKGLB closed to passenger traffic on 30 September 1957 and to freight 10 days later.

Opposite: (4) The Salzkammergut-Lokalbahn's powerful former German Military Railways 0-10-0TT No. 22, built by Borsig in 1939, stands at Bad Ischl with a train for Salzburg on the rainy 24 July 1956. Acquired by the SKGLB in December 1945, No. 22 was a valuable member of the locomotive fleet. PG0877

Above: (5) Two of the line's elegant Krauss, Linz 0-6-2Ts, No. 4 of 1890 and No. 11 of 1894, cross at St Wolfgang on 24 July 1956. A total of 10 examples of this class were built for the SKGLB between 1890 and 1906, and they were the line's predominant motive power until closure. PG0879

Above: (6) In another view on the unseasonably wet 24 July 1956, 0-6-2T No. 10, built by Krauss, Linz in 1893, stands at St Wolfgang with a train for Bad Ischl. PG0882

Opposite: (7) On 7 September 1958, almost a year after closure, 0-6-0T No. 30, seen with coach No. 566, awaits the cutter's torch at the former Salzburg Itzling works. No 30 and sister locomotive No 31, both built by Orenstein & Koppel in 1940, were used mainly on the branch from St Lorenz to Mondsee, and for shunting at the Salzburg end of the line. PG1544

Zillertalbahn

The Zillertalbahn, a 20½ mile (32.9km) 760mm gauge line between Jenbach and Mayrhofen, was built to connect the settlements along the Ziller valley with the standard gauge main line at Jenbach, opening in stages between 1900 and 1902.

(8) Zillertalbahn 0-6-2T No. 1, built by Krauss, Linz in 1900, a member of the widespread Austrian 'U' class, is seen at Jenbach on 31 July 1956. PG0909

(9) Zillertalbahn No. 3, an enlarged two cylinder compound version of the 'U' class design, built by Krauss, Linz in 1902, stands in the loop at Schlitters on 31 July 1956 with a train for Mayrhofen. PG0912

(10) The view forward from the rear of a typical Zillertalbahn mixed train from Mayrhofen to Jenbach, hauled by 0-6-2T No. 1 on 31 July 1956. PG911

(11) The original No. 4 of the Zillertalbahn, seen taking water at Jenbach shed in 1956, was an unusual 2-4-0T compound, built by Krauss, Linz in 1905. It was withdrawn from service in 1958 and sent for scrap in part exchange for No 22 of the SKGLB, which had closed the previous year. PG0916

(12) No. 2, a further 'U' class locomotive dating from 1900, is seen in profile at Jenbach on 12 September 1958. PG1635

(13) Not long after its arrival on the line, the Zillertalbahn's second No. 4, running without its tender, is seen shunting one of the line's traditional four-wheel coaches at Jenbach on 12 September 1958. PG1637

(14) Ten-coupled Borsig No. 4 runs light engine to Jenbach shed in the late afternoon sunshine. Built for the German military in 1939, the former Salzkammergut-Lokalbahn No. 22 had been made redundant by the closure of the SKGLB the previous year. PG1638

(15) On the evening of 12 September 1958, Zillertalbahn No. 2 has reached Uderns with the 5.45pm from Jenbach. The first coach, one of the line's impressive bogie observation carriages, has been occupied by the RCTS tour party. PG1640

Achenseebahn

The Achenseebahn, a metre gauge rack railway using the Riggenbach system, was opened in 1889, running from the main line station at Jenbach to Seespitz am Achensee, a distance of 4¼ miles (6.7km).

Opposite: (16) Achenseebahn No. 1, one of four locomotives built for the line by Floridsdorf in 1889, is seen at Jenbach on 12 September 1958. PG1625

Above: (17) Having propelled its train the 2¼ miles (3.6km) from Jenbach on gradients as steep as 1 in 6.25 (16%), No. 1 takes water at Eben, the summit of the line. Its train consists of one of the original open coaches supplied for the opening of the line. PG1628

(18) No. 1 has run round its single-coach train, and awaits departure from Eben. The locomotive will haul its train on the gently graded section of line from Eben to Seespitz am Achensee. PG1629

(19) Achenseebahn No. 1 pauses at Maurach, 3 miles from Jenbach. It will shortly continue its journey to Seespitz, where it will connect with the lake steamer services. PG1630

Left: (20) No. 1 is seen from the train on the return journey, descending the incline towards Jenbach in the evening sun. PG1633

Opposite: (21) The dependable 'U' class 0-6-2Ts were used extensively on the Steiermärkische Landesbahnen's narrow gauge lines. No. U7, built by Krauss, Linz in 1899, has arrived at Unzmarkt on the morning of 5 September 1963. PG3491

Murtalbahn (StmLB)

The 760mm gauge Murtalbahn opened in 1894, running 47½ miles (76.2km) from Unzmarkt, where it connected with the standard gauge main line, to Mauterndorf. For many years, the image of the Murtalbahn was defined by its 0-6-2T 'U' class locomotives, with their distinctive spark arrester chimneys, which were the line's standard motive power until dieselisation in the 1960s.

Above: (22) Built for the Feistritztalbahn in 1930, No. Kh 111 was transferred to the Murtalbahn in 1943. The Caprotti valve gear fitted 0-10-0T stands at Unzmarkt with a two-coach RCTS special on 5 September 1963. PG3492

Opposite: (23) No. Kh 111 is seen en route from Unzmarkt to Murau with the RCTS train. PG3494

(24) The operational centre of the line was located at Murau, 16¾ miles (26.9km) from Unzmarkt. No. U9, built for the opening of the Murtalbahn by Krauss, Linz in 1894, originally No. 9 *Murau*, stands outside Murau shed. PG3497

(25) After arrival with the RCTS special, No. Kh111 is seen at the depot at Murau, standing beside No. U11, with No. U9 in the background.
PG3498

(26) No. U11, another of the original Murtalbahn locomotives of 1894, originally No. 11 *Mauterndorf*, stands at Murau-Stolzalpe station with the RCTS special on 5 September 1963. PG3499

Gleisdorf - Weiz (StmLB)

The 9½ mile long (15km) standard gauge line from Gleisdorf to Weiz opened in 1889, with the Steiermärkische Landesbahnen taking over its operation in 1922. Until dieselisation in 1964/65 it operated an interesting selection of steam locomotives obtained from a variety of sources.

(27) On 3 September 1963 Steiermärkische Landesbahnen 2-6-2T No. 130.03, an SLM product of 1905, is seen at Wollsdorf at the head of a train from Gleisdorf to Weiz. PG3452

(28) No. 130.03, seen on arrival at Weiz, and its sister No. 130.04, originally Nos. 43 and 44 of the Gürbetalbahn in Switzerland, were sold to the BBÖ in Austria in 1921, from where the StmLB acquired them a few years later. After many years on the Gleisdorf - Weiz line, No. 130.04 was withdrawn in 1957 and 130.03 in 1965. PG3453

(29) 0-8-0T No. 178.02, built by Krauss, Linz in 1923, and seen at Weiz shed on 3 September 1963, was withdrawn three years later. PG3454

Feistritztalbahn (StmLB)

The Feistritztalbahn was another Steiermärkische Landesbahnen 760mm gauge line. Opened in 1911, it ran from Weiz, where it connected with the standard gauge line from Gleisdorf, 15 miles (23.9km) to Birkfeld. The line was extended by 11½ miles (18.3km) from Birkfeld to Ratten in 1922, but would be cut back to Birkfeld again in the early 1970s.

Opposite: (30) The Steiermärkische Landesbahnen acquired three of the former Salzkammergut-Lokalbahn's attractive 0-6-2Ts after its closure in 1957. All three were modified by the StmLB with extended side tanks. No. S7, built by Krauss, Linz in 1893, formerly SKGLB No. 7, stands outside Weiz shed on 3 September 1963. PG3456

Above: (31) Another former Salzkammergut-Lokalbahn locomotive, No. S12, built by Krauss, Linz in 1906, formerly SKGLB No. 12, waits at Weiz on 3 September 1958 with the RCTS special. PG3458

Above: (32) Smartly turned out No. S12 is the centre of attention at Weiz as it awaits departure with the RCTS special on the Feistritztalbahn. The distinctive chimney marks it out as a former Salzkammergut-Lokalbahn locomotive. PG3457

Opposite: (33) A view from the footplate of No. S12 on its way up the valley. PG3462

(34) The station layout at Birkfeld is seen from the footplate of No. S12. PG3463

(35) StmLB No. 699.01 was built as a 0-8-0TT for the German *Heeresfeldbahn* by Franco-Belge in 1944 as No. HF 2855. In 1946 it became SKGLB No. 19, but it was sold to the Steiermärkische Landesbahnen in 1955, and rebuilt at Weiz as a tank locomotive. On 3 September 1963 it pauses at Birkfeld with a train for Weiz. Out of use by 1965, it was sold to the Welshpool & Llanfair Railway in 1969. PG3464

(36) No. S12 stands outside the attractive shed at Ratten at the end of its journey from Weiz. PG3465

Lokalbahn Kapfenberg - Au-Seewiesen (StmLB)

Opened in 1893, the 760mm gauge line from Kapfenberg to Au-Seewiesen, 14 miles (22.7km) distant, was also known as the Thörlerbahn. Regular passenger services ended in 1959, but the line remained open for freight traffic, serving the important local iron & steel and timber industries, although the last two miles (3km) from Seebach-Turnau to Au-Seewiesen closed in 1964.

(37) 0-6-0T No. 6 *Thörl*, built by Krauss, Linz in 1893 for the opening of the line, is seen with a special train at Kapfenberg on 30 August 1964. PG3883

Opposite: (38) No. 6 *Thörl* is seen posed on a roadside section of line with the special train. PG3886

Above: (39) Whilst two of the Steiermärkische Landesbahnen's ex-SKGLB 0-6-2Ts were employed on the Feistritztalbahn, the third - No. 11 of 1894, seen at Kapfenberg in August 1964 - operated on the Thörlerbahn from 1958 to 1967. PG3884

Right: (40) The line's only tunnel, less than 30ft long, was at Thörl, seven miles (11.5km) from Kapfenberg. The special emerges from the tunnel on a photographic run-past. PG3887

Pinzgauer Lokalbahn (ÖBB)

The 760mm gauge Pinzgauer Lokalbahn, also known as the Krimmler Bahn, was opened in 1898. It ran 33 miles (52.7km) from the standard gauge main line station at Zell am See along the valley of the river Salzach to Krimml. The depot was situated at Tischlerhäusl, one mile (1.5km) from Zell am See station.

(41) On 11 September 1958, the RCTS tour visited the ÖBB's Pinzgauer Lokalbahn. Seen from the third coach, Class 298 No. 298.05, built by Krauss, Linz in 1898, hauls a train conveying the RCTS party from Zell am See to Krimml. PG1613

Above: (42) Nos. 298.51 and 298.56 stand at the depot at Tischlerhäusl, where both locomotives were based for many years until being transferred to Garsten shed on the Steyrtalbahn, in 1961 and 1960 respectively. PG1622

Right: (43) No. 298.05 runs round its train at the sizeable terminus at Krimml. No 298.05 left the Pinzgauer Lokalbahn for the Steyrtalbahn in May 1963. PG1615

(44) Seen at Tischlerhäusl, ÖBB No. 998.01, built by Krauss, München in 1920, was the only member of its class. Built for the Kreuznacher Kleinbahnen in Germany, it moved to Austrian territory during World War 2. It subsequently passed into ÖBB stock and operated on the Pinzgauer Lokalbahn until the 1960s. PG1620

(45) Class 498 superheated 0-6-2T No. 498.08 is seen at Tischlerhäusl. The ÖBB had eight of these locomotives, which were built between 1928 and 1931 as the final development of the 'U' class. Despite their relative modernity they were all out of service by the late 1960s. No. 498.08 left the Pinzgauer Lokalbahn for Garsten in 1963. PG1623

(46) Amongst various narrow gauge locomotives left at the Pinzgauer Lokalbahn at the end of World War 2 was this small industrial 0-4-0WT, built by Krauss, München in 1903, seen standing derelict at Tischlerhäusl. PG1621

Gurktalbahn (ÖBB)

The 760mm gauge Gurktalbahn was opened in 1898. Connecting with the standard gauge main line at Treibach-Althofen, it ran a distance of 18 miles (28.8km) along the valley of the river Gurk to Klein Glödnitz. Passenger services were withdrawn in 1968 and the line was cut back to Gurk, 10½ miles (17km) from Treibach-Althofen, with limited freight operations continuing until early 1972. A two-mile (3km) section would survive as Austria's first preserved railway.

(47) ÖBB Class 199 0-8-2T No. 199.02 stands in the rain at Treibach-Althofen with the RCTS special train on 5 September 1963. PG3501

(48) No. 199.02, built by Krauss, Linz for the BBÖ in 1926, stands with its train after arriving at the terminus of Klein Glödnitz. PG3503

(49) A portrait of No. 199.02 at Klein Glödnitz. Nos. 199.02 and 199.03 both spent several years on the Gurktalbahn until being transferred to the Vellachtalbahn in 1968. PG3504

Vellachtalbahn (ÖBB)

The 760mm gauge Vellachtalbahn, opened in 1902, ran 11 miles (17.5km) from the main line station at Völkermarkt-Kühnsdorf to the terminus at Eisenkappel. Passenger services were withdrawn in January 1965, and the line was cut back to Rechberg, 9 miles (14km) from Völkermarkt-Kühnsdorf, with freight services continuing until road improvements led to final closure in May 1971.

(50) ÖBB Class 699.1 0-8-0T No. 699.103, a former *Heeresfeldbahn* German military railway locomotive built by Franco-Belge in 1944, stands at Miklauzhof with the RCTS special on 6 September 1963. PG3507

(51) The RCTS train has reached the terminus of the line at Eisenkappel. No 699.103 was one of seven former *Heeresfeldbahn* Class KDL 11 locomotives inherited by the ÖBB after World War 2, of which four were rebuilt as tank locomotives, and subsequently fitted with Giesl ejectors in the 1950s. No. 699.103 was originally *Heeresfeldbahn* No. HF 2821. PG3509

(52) Hauling the combined RCTS special and service trains, Nos. 699.103 and 699.01 run beside the river Vellach between Eisenkappel and Miklauzhof on the return journey to Völkermarkt-Kühnsdorf. PG3513

(53) Nos. 699.103 and 699.01 pause at Miklauzhof on the return working. Just visible at the rear of the train are standard gauge wagons on 760mm gauge transporter wagons, which had been attached at the paper mill at Rechberg. PG3514

(54) Seen after arrival at Völkermarkt-Kühnsdorf, Nos. 699.01 and 699.103 show the very different outlines of the Class 699 0-8-0TT and the Giesl ejector equipped Class 699.1 0-8-0T. After the Vellachtalbahn closed in 1971 No. 699.103 was transferred to the Steyrtalbahn, where it operated until the demise of that line. PG3515

Steyrtalbahn (ÖBB)

The Steyrtalbahn, Austria's first 760mm gauge line, opened in stages between 1889 and 1909 from Garsten to Klaus, a total distance of 25 miles (39.8km). A branch from Pergern to Bad Hall opened in 1891, but was cut back to just 3 miles (4.8km) in 1933, and closed completely in 1967. Passenger services were replaced by buses between Molln and Klaus in 1968, and the line was closed completely between Grünburg and Klaus in 1980. The remaining Garsten - Grünburg section closed two years later, with the line between Steyr and Grünburg subsequently being preserved.

(55) Class 298 0-6-2T No. 298.53, built by Krauss, Linz in 1898, is seen shunting at Garsten on 7 September 1963. The locomotive depot lies just out of site around the curve to the left. PG3538

(56) A view of Garsten shed on 7 September 1963, with three members of Class 298 visible. On the left is No. 298.56, built by Floridsdorf in 1900. The 'U' class, which became ÖBB Class 298, was a development of the original Steyrtalbahn locomotives. PG3539

(57) Class 298.1 No. 298.105, with a Garsten - Klaus train conveying the RCTS party, is seen taking water at Grünburg on the evening of 7 September 1963. No 298.105, another Krauss, Linz product, was originally Steyrtalbahn No. 5 *Letten* of 1891, and was withdrawn in December 1965. PG3540

Waldviertelbahn (ÖBB)

The Waldviertelbahn consisted of two sections. The northern line, opened in 1900, ran 16 miles (25.4km) from Gmünd to Litschau, with an 8¼ mile (13.2km) branch from Alt Nagelberg to Heidenreichstein. The southern line opened as far as Steinbach-Groß Pertholz in 1902, and was extended the following year to its terminus at Groß Gerungs, 27 miles (43km) from Gmünd.

(58) ÖBB Class 299 No. 299.02, stored at Gmünd shed on 1 September 1963, was one of a pair of Class Mv two-cylinder compound Engerths built by Krauss, Linz in 1907, which spent many years on the Waldviertelbahn. No. 299.02 was officially withdrawn the following year. PG3415

(59) Class 598 No. 598.02 was the second of three two-cylinder compound 0-6-4Ts built in 1896 as Class Yv for the Ybbstalbahn, where they spent nearly all their working lives. No. 598.02 moved to Gmünd with sister locomotive 598.03 in 1962, but their use on the Waldviertelbahn was short-lived, and both were out of service by 1964. PG3416

(60) Class 399 No. 399.06 was the last built of the highly successful superheated Class Mh Engerth design, supplied for use on the steeply graded Mariazellerbahn. No. 399.06, built by Krauss, Linz in 1908, is seen in company with the first two examples of the class, Nos. 399.01 and 399.02 of 1906. PG3418

(61) No. 598.02 stands at the narrow gauge station platform at Gmünd with the RCTS special to Groß Gerungs on 1 September 1963. The standard gauge station was on the opposite side of the main road, behind the trees to the right of the picture. PG3424

Above: (62) No. 598.02 is seen en route to Groß Gerungs. The unusual trailing bogie, a feature which was unique to Class 598 on the Austrian narrow gauge, is clearly visible. PG3426

Right: (63) No. 598.02 is seen from the train on the return working from Groß Gerungs to Gmünd. The formation consists of typical Austrian narrow gauge four-wheel coaches with end balconies. PG3430

Obergrafendorf (ÖBB)

Obergrafendorf, situated a few miles south of St Pölten on the 760mm gauge Mariazellerbahn, possessed extensive sidings and a large locomotive depot with turntable. From 1958 onwards the redundant depot sidings were used to house a large number of out of service ÖBB narrow gauge steam locomotives, which would often spend several years in store before final withdrawal.

(64) Amongst the various locomotives present at Obergrafendorf in September 1963 were Nos. 399.03 and 298.205. No. 399.03 would soon return to service on the Waldviertelbahn, where it was reunited with the other members of Class 399. No. 298.205, built in 1902 as a member of Class Uh, had last operated on the Ybbstalbahn in 1962, and would eventually be restored to use on the preserved section of the Ybbstalbahn in 2001. PG3439

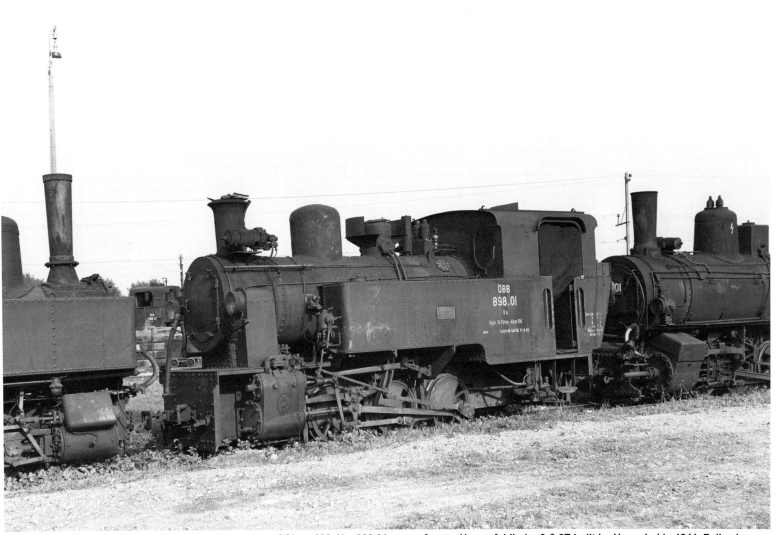

(65) Also present in September 1963, the only member of Class 898, No. 898.01, was a former Heeresfeldbahn 0-6-0T built by Henschel in 1941. Following a period on static display, No. 898.01 was acquired by the preserved Gurktalbahn and restored to working order in 1998. Behind it can be seen compound Engerth No. 299.01, sister of No. 299.02 seen in picture 58 at Gmünd. Sadly No. 299.01 would not run again. PG3440

Schafbergbahn (ÖBB)

The Schafbergbahn was opened in 1893 as a metre gauge rack railway using the Abt system, running from the lakeside resort of St Wolfgang to the summit of the Schafberg in the Salzkammergut region of lakes and mountains east of Salzburg.

(66) From its opening the Schafbergbahn was operated by six rack tank locomotives supplied by Krauss, Linz as Nos Z1 - Z6. The original No Z2, now running as ÖBB No. 999.102, awaits its next duty at St Wolfgang on 24 July 1956. PG0880

(67) No. 999.106, originally No Z6, is seen at St Wolfgang on the same date. By 1955, all members of Class 999.1 had been fitted with Giesl ejectors, their purpose being less to improve the locomotives' performance than to reduce the risk of them throwing sparks on their journey up the mountain. No. 999.106 would be transferred from St Wolfgang to Puchberg in 1974 to supplement the original five Schneebergbahn locomotives. PG0881

Schneebergbahn (ÖBB)

Running from the town of Puchberg am Schneeberg to the summit of the Schneeberg, the Schneebergbahn was opened in 1897, four years after the Schafbergbahn. It too was a metre gauge rack line built on the Abt system. Motive power consisted of five locomotives, very similar to those on the Schafbergbahn, built by Krauss, Linz between 1897 and 1900, and numbered Z1 - Z5.

(68) Originally supplied as Nos. Z4 and Z2, ÖBB Class 999 locomotives Nos. 999.04 and 999.02 stand outside Puchberg shed on 2 September 1963. PG3444

(69) No. 999.04 stands at Schneeberg summit on 11 September 1964. As on the Schafbergbahn, all of the Schneebergbahn locomotives were fitted with Giesl ejectors in the 1950s. PG3969

(70) No. 999.04 is making its way to the summit at Hochschneeberg on 11 September 1964. Positioned in front of the single coach is a water wagon. These were taken to stations along the line to provide a supply from which locomotives could take water during their ascent. PG3971

(71) No. 999.04 is seen at rest at Puchberg shed with a classmate. PG3973

Graz-Köflacher Bahn

The Graz-Köflacher Bahn was built to serve the coalfields to the west of Graz. The 25½ mile (41km) main line from Graz to Köflach opened in 1860, followed in 1873 by a line from a junction at Lieboch to Wies-Eibiswald, 31½ miles (50.7km) distant. From 1930 the GKB took over operation of the Sulmtalbahn from Leibnitz to Pölfing-Brunn, where it connected with the GKB line from Lieboch. The GKB was notable during the 1950s and 1960s for its fleet of veteran ex-main line steam locomotives.

(72) GKB No. 372, seen at Graz GKB shed on 9 September 1958, was a member of Südbahn Class 17c, built by Floridsdorf in 1891. Acquired by the GKB in 1924, it was not withdrawn until May 1968. PG1578

(73) Seen at Graz shed on the same day, two-cylinder compound 2-8-0 No. 56.3195 was built by Wiener Neustadt in 1917 as kkStB No 170.492, and purchased in December 1951 by the GKB, where it operated for a further 20 years until withdrawal in 1971. PG1577

(74) No. 372, seen at Graz GKB station with a long rake of empty stock on the evening of 9 September 1958, was one of eight members of Class 17c acquired by the GKB in 1924/25. PG1580

(75) *Sulm 2*, formerly No. 30.39, seen at Leibnitz on 4 September 1963, was one of 13 members of Class 30, a two-cylinder compound 2-6-2T, acquired by the GKB in the 1930s. PG3469

(76) *Sulm 2* at Leibnitz, with the 7.55am mixed train to Wies-Eibiswald, was one of two Class 30 locomotives which were allocated to Sulmtalbahn services by the GKB in the 1950s, and given new identities as *Sulm 1* and *Sulm 2*. PG3468

(77) *Sulm 2* stands at Wies-Eibiswald with the 7.55am from Leibnitz on 4 September 1963. Partly because of time spent shunting en route, the train was allowed some two hours for the journey from Leibnitz, with a timetabled arrival time of 10am. PG3472

(78) Class 17c No. 372 stands at Wies-Eibiswald, terminus of the line from Lieboch, with the RCTS train on 4 September 1963. PG3475

(79) Recently ex-works No. 671 stands at Köflach, terminus of the line from Graz. Between 1924 and 1926 the GKB acquired 18 members of Class 29. Although most were withdrawn in the 1930s, four survived in service until the 1960s. No. 671 was never officially withdrawn, and is still used on special duties, having been restored in the 1970s. PG3478

(80) No. 671, built by StEG for the Südbahn in 1860 as a member of Class 29, is seen at Premstätten-Tobelbad with an RCTS special from Köflach to Graz on 4 September 1963. PG3482

(81) No. 56.3268, built by Wiener Neustadt in 1919 as No. 170.679, stands at Graz with the stock for an evening train to Wies-Eibiswald on 4 September 1963. It was acquired by the GKB in 1951, and operated there until 1970. PG3486

(82) No. 56.3268 departs Graz for Wies-Eibiswald, passing No. 671. A total of 16 members of Class 56 were acquired by the GKB between 1948 and 1955, and they dominated freight operations until the arrival of former ÖBB 2-10-0s of Class 50 and Class 152 between 1968 and 1973. PG3488

(83) A final view of former Südbahn Class 17c 4-4-0 No. 372 of 1891, at the head of a packed train of 10 four-wheel coaches and a van at Graz GKB station on 9 September 1958. No. 372 survives in preservation, and was restored to working order in 2005. PG1588